Full Marks *for trying* Fenton-Ryder

This is the story of one David Fenton-Ryder, whom Fate had appointed should spend his formative years at a well-known school called Bishop Petre. Under the tutelage of various Masters, he eventually learns the ways of the world and leaves the school in a blaze of self-appointed glory. However, the road to success was sometimes long and arduous and filled with misunderstandings and misgivings, especially on the part of his long-suffering Housemaster, Anthony Baigent.

This book is the result of the inspiration of several authors. Two Masters of Wanganui Collegiate School, Reverend A. Sangster and Mr I.M. Davis, and one of the House Tutors, His Royal Highness the Prince Edward, were assisted in their creation by two boys of the school, Francis Cooke and Edward Abraham. The resulting text was admirably illustrated by the pen (mightier than the sword) of another Collegiate student, Blair Mainwaring.

For the purposes of authenticity, this history of the exploits of David Fenton-Ryder is traced through a series of letters, with reports, memos and narrative employed to help the poor reader cope with the subtleties of Our Hero's fertile imagination.

To help explain some of the mysteries of private school education to the uninitiated, there is a glossary on page 112.

FULL MARKS, *for trying* Fenton-Ryder!

H.R.H. The Prince Edward   Rev. A. Sangster
Mr I. M. Davis
Francis Cooke   Edward Abraham
assisted by Max Fretter of the lowly third

illustrated by Blair Mainwaring

HALE · LONDON

© 1983 Collegiate School

First published in Great Britain 1983
Reprinted 1983
Robert Hale Limited
Clerkenwell House
Clerkenwell Green
London EC1

ISBN 0 7090 1231 4 (*paperback*)
ISBN 0 7090 1460 0 (*hard cover*)

Printed and bound in Great Britain by
Redwood Burn Ltd., Trowbridge, Wiltshire

COLLEGIATE SCHOOL
WANGANUI

Sometimes only the serious side of school life is evident and yet as with most things with which we are associated there is the amusing. This young man, Fenton-Ryder, reminds us of that fact and possibly even more.

When George Bernard Shaw's "Pygmalion" was first performed the audience laughed uproariously. It was only later they realized at whom they had been laughing.

I know that Masters and boys, parents and others will thoroughly enjoy the progress of this school-boy.

I warmly congratulate the contributors on capturing, albeit in a somewhat embellished way, some not entirely unusual events and comments.

1 April 1983

I.D. McKinnon
Headmaster

David Fenton-Ryder

Portrait of Our Hero in his First Year, resolved to assault the novel experience of Bishop Petre School with fortitude, boldness and valour, and totally un- daunted by the alarming accounts of those Great Men who have gone before. Equipped with every artifice and strategem, the future holds no fear for Our Hero.

Portrait of Our Hero's intimate ally (and sometime most bitter adversary), who is endowed with many insignificant virtues such as intelligence and intellect, but who often demonstrates great allegiance when it is safe so to do.

Herbert

1 Our Hero's first letter home, his first accomplished prep, and his esteemed Housemaster's polite letter. His letter astonished his parents, his prep astounded his masters, and the House-master's letter was no surprise to anyone.

Seafield House
Bishop Petre School
Wanganui

January 10th ,1979

Dear Mr Fenton-Ryder,

I am delighted to see that David's name appears on my list of newboys for this year; reference to the School Register shows that David will be a third generation Fenton-Ryder to come to Seafield. The Register also records that grandfather and father were both members of the 1st XI, which suggests that Seafield's Minor House team will have at least one promising member in '79.

Naturally I would very much like to meet both you and your wife when you bring David to school on February 2nd, and I suggest that you call at my house at around 2:15.

David, I believe, has been to Prep School as a boarder for the past three years, so he should have little difficulty settling down here. Furthermore there are two others from his present school coming to Seafield with him, which should make things easier for him.

My wife and I look forward very much to meeting you both on February 2nd.

Yours sincerely,

Anthony Baspent.

Seafield House

Wanganui

Dear Mum and Dad,
Thank-you for the letter and the $5:00. Can you write again because I had too spend the money on a new pen because my new freind, Herb, bent the nib in a ~~sifffff~~ sience lesson when he stuck it up a gas tap, I got told off by the sience Master cause he said I left the gas tap on — but it wazn't me — Herbert did it and coodn't turn it off so he stuck my pen up the pipe to stop the gas coming out. The science Master is always miserable and ~~scowls~~ all the time when I come in the room, my ~~freind~~ freind Herbert got me off on the wrong fot especially since I ~~fagot~~ my last Prep, and said that ~~gas gassed~~ gas-tube (thats his nick name) I'd be ~~tube~~ WHACKED ..... ~~grace~~ grace for us new boys grace ends tomorrow..! &

The Housemaster is called Borax by us boys, and Herbert didn't know that and he went up to Borax and said I've been sent to report to Borax, you shoud have seen his face, Herbert tryed to blame me but I was put up to it, by a senior dorm prefect called 'Wriggles', Borax wasn't so nice to me after Dad went home. Mrs Baigent (Mrs Borax) said that your hair looked BEAUTIFIL and I said that you like it to and spend hours bleaching it.

I tried to join the rowing but they wont let me so I just have to play silly Hexcad's running about in soccer or non-stop cricket while GOD (chaplain) ~~yans~~ yawns & smokes his pipe, and pretends hes interested. God is sometimes nice, but he hit me with a Bible the other day cos I ~~asked~~ asked if Goliath was an Arab terrorist. He preached a long sermon on SIN on Sunday, he said he's against it and he sweated all the time he preached. God told all the parents that he wouldn't force us to be confirmed and today he said we would all be confirmed in June. He hit herbert when herbert said he was an athnostic, or something like that. I think Herbert's very clever.

My Piano teacher is no better than my last one and has put me back onto Book I. I don't think he can play the piano himself. The prefects seem all right at the moment but the Headmaster told them to be good to us new boys and he's pretty fierce all the time. In Big school assembly he gets very angry all the time, the second years bet on how long he will carry on. At least when he's very cross it eats into the first period and that's Latin. Why do we have to do Latin?? I wrote in my text-book "Latin is a subject as dead as dead can be, first it killed the Romans and now its killing me." we all thought that was very funny. but I'm afraid Ego Smith (my latin teacher) is going to put the bill on your account. sorry about that. I must finish now because "gas-tube" has come back into the class. Don't forget

Some more money please

Give my love to Hercules (don't forget to feed him)

David

'God'

Portrait of the much 'beloved' Chaplain equipped with his two
most horrendous weapons: the one for fumigating Big School,
the other for assaulting sinful boys who disagree with him. This
battery weapon holds great terror to all within his reach or aim
and so accounts for why Our Hero always sits at the back of
the class.

me permishing making Herbet for splodges

D. Fenton-Ryder

WHY I LIKE SCHOOL

School is very likeabull.... ~~H~~ I like school a lot. It is fun to watch. ~~Old Borax~~ The Housemaster blow a fuze at peple and ~~thing to stop~~ the period's continuing is very entertaining. Prep time is also esciting but most of all I like the ~~dormitrys~~ dormitorys after ~~lites~~ lights out. The only thing I dont like about school is ~~Old Borax~~ the teacher's who think they know everything but don't kno ~~that~~ it is nearly always Herbet's fault and not mine.

I like the dining-hall. The only thing I dont like about the dining-hall is the ~~food~~ but the Dining-hall is ~~asthetiles~~ astheticaly pleasing and would be a good place to eat a good meal in. I think the tost is well cooked: It could be dried and used for patio tiles as it would never wear out and the baked ~~patotoo~~ make excellent cricket balls.

~~Asthew~~ Actuly, sport is very enjoyable and gives a marvelous feeling. The only sport I deteste is Hexads, which is the only sport I ~~play~~ am allowed to play

So obviously. School is very ~~likeable~~ like a bull Ha ha ha
This is a joak

P.S sorry it is three days late. I kept forgetting to hand it in. Also Herbet made the splodges and not me.

2 Our Hero starts to find his feet and his Housemaster starts to lose his head. A letter from Our Hero's Father instructing his progeny in the finer virtues of life; Our Hero's letter preparing his dear parents for his first assessment report; and finally the odious document itself.

Portrait of Borax in characteristic posture (and mood) preparing to instruct Our Hero in the finer acts of discipline.

Seafield House
Bishop Petre School
Wanganui

March 1st, 1979

Dear Mr Fenton-Ryder,

I am sorry that you were unable to come over for the New Boys' weekend, but David explained that you had to be in Wellington at the time, as you had a horse running at Trentham.

I am, therefore, writing this note to let you know how David is settling down after his first few weeks here.

He has had rather a set-back over rowing. It seems that he was under the impression that he would be accepted immediately into the Rowing Club, and was very disappointed to learn that he could not apply until the third term. He seems to have settled into Hexads happily now, and is making an enthusiastic contribution in this competition.

In the House he is starting to learn our ways, but he tends to be very forgetful, and this has meant that he has had rather too many minor punishments since coming off "grace".

This failing has been commented upon by his masters. David has on more than one occasion forgotten to do his prep, and too often has handed up poorly presented and insufficient work. As a consequence he has had a number of "repeats".

He seems to be getting on well with others of his age group in the House and has made a number of new friends.

I trust he is keeping you well informed with regular letters. My regards to Mrs Fenton-Ryder.

Yours sincerely,

Anthony Baipent.

GLENDALE STATION
GORDONSDOWN
New Zealand

Feb 14th, 1979

My Dear Boy,

There is great honour attached to Bishop Petre School,
and by attaching yourself to the School, I expect you to
be attached to the honour. Be proud of the School and
of the Family Name. Fenton-Ryders have always been
proud of their School - and their School has always been
proud of them. We have served them on the sports field -
your dear late Grandfather and I were both members of
the Cricket XI and the First XV - and neither of us ever
missed a tackle. Rowing, however, is NOT a Fenton-Ryder
sport. Rowers are clumsy, ungainly boys. Cricketers
are real, courageous men.

To the point, your Housemaster appears to view you in
an unfavourable light. He has accused you of many
things which I, personally, find difficult to believe.
Please, Fenton-Ryder - don't DO things I find difficult
to believe!

Your Mother intends you to do well at the piano. Well,
of course, do your best - but FIRST develop a good eye
for the ball - ESSENTIALS FIRST!!

Father

Seafield House
Wanganui

Dear Mum and Dad,
We had an assessment report this week, I did very well ~ in sport, I got a B, also I got a C in games. The rest of my subject were pretty average. The masters think I'm working very hard all and Dug Murphy our English Master said if I worked a little harder I would get a university degree or something in 20 years. Smasher Smith is the P.E Master, he got very angry with Herbert the other day because Herbert threw a cricket ball through a gym window. He gave me a whack with the sandshoe too just because I was standing next to Herbert. If you hear about this don't say I told you but you will know what happened. Thank-you for the knew pen but could you send me some more pocket-money I want to buy my OWN Bible. Herbert got all B's in his subjects but he can be a bit of a creep. Fergusson and Ginger from my old prep school are still here, which is a shame, they don't like the school cause they aint any good at sport. Ginger cries everytime a senior prefect speaks to him, and Fergusson has joined the Chapel Choir. Herbert put a WETA in his bed and he reported Herbert to the Choir master that was bad cause we all got into trouble for that. All my prep is being done on time though once or twice I forgot to hand it in cos I'm so busy.
love
Dave

P.S. Don't forget to look after Hercules

the Weta !!!

Deplorable portrait of Our Hero's contemporaries, significant only in so far that the officious and meddling master-in-charge displaced Our Hero from his rightful front-centre row place on the mere despicable grounds that he forgot his shoes and socks.

THIRD FORM ASSESSMENT REPORT

A = Excellent B = Very Good/Good C = Average only D = Below Average
E = Well Below Average

ENGLISH D Prep late everytime: has to be watched all the time. P.F.M.

MATHEMATICS D. Some ability though I suspect he has managed to obtain an answer book to our text book. JVB

FRENCH E UNDER THE IMPRESSION YOU ONLY NEED TO STUDY FRENCH IF YOU INTEND TO HAVE A FRENCH MISTRESS! CM

LATIN D classwork weak — still waiting to see his prep. M.J.S.

HISTORY D. Still thinks King Arthur fought the Persians! JMW.

GEOGRAPHY D Seems attentive in class but prep sloppy PBT.

SCIENCE e No effort made — under the impression that apparatus is supplied for his personal entertainment. BLH.

PHYS. ED. B Little skill, but highly aggressive & competitive. BRS

GAMES C Needs screwing to the floor. P.F.M.

OTHER COMMENTS Who let him in?! J.V.B.

Trying — very, at all times P.B.C.

Pictorial account of the odious 'incident' in which Our Unfortunate Hero was compelled to defend his person by projecting a stool at his assailant thus accidently demolishing a prep-room door.

3 Several views of a confusing and complex calamity in which, according to Our Hero, he is abused by his best friend, misunderstood by a senior prefect and totally misinterpreted by his Housemaster.

Seafield House

Bishop Petre School

Wanganui

March 12th,1979

Dear Mr Fenton-Ryder,

I am sorry to say that young David got himself involved in a stupid incident earlier in the week, and I feel that you should know about it.

From my inquiries it would seem that David got into an argument with two others of his year in the Prep Room. The exchange became heated and noisy to the point where one of the boys tore up a repeat which David had just completed. David in retaliation, and in a fit of anger, picked up a stool and threw it at the offender. It missed, but went crashing through the glass panel of the Prep Room door. Unfortunately one of the prefects, hearing the noise, was coming through the door to find out what was going on. He was cut about the face and had to receive three stitches in his cheek.

I had David in, and he agreed that the facts which I have related were correct. I caned him, made it very clear to him that he must control himself better in the future, and informed him that he must pay for a new pane of glass out of his pocket money.

I am sorry that I should have to write this letter. David is a good lad, but he must learn to curb this precipitate side to his nature.

My regards to Mrs Fenton-Ryder.

Yours sincerely,

Anthony Baird.

<u>Prefects Written Report to Housemaster.</u>

Sir,

Fenton-Ryder has caused me to speak to him 5-6 times during every prep. He has been on drills and tardy this week and generally obnoxious when other boys are trying to do their prep. He gets so many repeats that his desk is full of work still to do. On the evening in question he flicked ink-pellets at nearly everyone in the dorm, and when Smith retaliated they landed up tearing one another's books up and throwing rulers at one another. I was walking into the room to quieten things down when Fenton-Ryder who was standing on Smith's desk shouting he was king of (~~   ~~)the Castle threw the stool through the door and so cut my face. It was then he fell off his desk and banged his nose He has apologised to me.

F. Cooke

"Fanny Cooke"

*henceforth known as Scarface!!

Seafield House
Wanganui

Dear Mummy,
You may hear from Borax soon that
I have been ~~accident~~ accidentally involved in a
bit of trouble which was really nothing to do with
me. You see I was doing my Latin prep in the
dorm when Herbert ~~flick~~ flicked ink all over my
book and shirt. He always gets me into that sort
of thing, and I told him that he shouldn't do that sort
me and tore my work up, they keep picking on me
because I'm doing so well in class. Anyway, cos
they were picking on me I had to defend myself
and they were threatening me with their rules so
I picked up my stool to stop them hitting me and it
slipped out of my hand and fell through the glass
door to the corridor. Unfortunately the door was
shut and it broke a bit of glass, the whole door
in fact, just as ~~funny~~ Cooke, the prefect, was
coming in to stop them all bullying me. He got
a little cut, nothing serious, just a little graze, you
could hardly see it, but they had to put three
~~stitches~~ stitches in his cheek. Old Borax was
Furious he never even tried to listen to my
side of the story — he said the stool couldn't
fall out of my hand horizontally for 6 metres —
but he didn't seem to understand that I was
being pushed back so fast by the bullies that the
stool fell out of my hand at speed :— if you see
what I mean. He gave me six strokes on the
rear and said he would right to you so I
thought I would tell you the real facts as
they happened. exactly. He's going to charge my
account $10.00 but that isn't fair so could
you get some money off Pad and send it quickly

2

because the Chaplain said he wants me
to have my own prayer book. Also the other
day I accidentally walked into a door and it
caused my nose to bleed but I slept with
the Matron. and I feel <u>much better</u> now.

Lots of love

Davi

Seafield House
Bishop Petre School
Wanganui

March 20th, 1979

Dear Mrs Fenton-Ryder,

Many thanks for your letter and the comments you made over the recent incident concerning David and his fight in the Prep Room.

I am sorry that David feels regret at being in the same House with two boys with whom he failed to get along at Prep School. I am sorry also that he feels that these two boys are 'taking it out of him' and are trying to get the other first years against him. Actually only one of the boys you mention in your letter was involved in the incident, the other was a boy who, I had been led to believe had become very friendly with David since they first met here in the House.

David's dormitory prefect is quite certain that the whole affair has blown over, but on my instructions he will keep a close watch, and will make every effort to get these young men to get along with one another more tolerantly.

I have handed the cheque you enclosed with your letter to the House Tutor, and it will be credited to David's bank account.

Thank you again for your letter, and my regards to your husband.

Yours sincerely,

Anthony Sarpent.

Seafield House,
Dorm 3, Bed No. 9.

Dear Mother and Father,
　　　　　　　　　How are you! I'm fine. Thank
you for the nice (at) cake, can you make them
bigger please. I think I'm settling down very
well but I can't say that for some of my
friends. Do you remember that horrible boy David
whom I talked about in my last letter, well
now he's more horrible. Last night I offered to
check his bad spelling in his repeat (which he
got from Digger). He said no, but he would check
my good spelling. I said no, then he tried to
get my (~~book~~) book and started (~~fighting me~~) to fight
me (he does not know that I have done boxing). He
got mad and ~~through~~ (through/throw) well like me can, and the chair
went through the glass door and it cut a profect
(he needed a (~~bandy~~) bondage) He is in trouble.
　　　　Class is going very well I have been told by
all my masters that I am a very good boy, I told
them I thought I was too. I hit a six in (~~cricket~~
cricket) My violin is also good apart from David
who tries to play piano and is very awful
and ~~disturbs~~ disturbs me all the time.
Please put more cherries in the cake.

　　　　　　　　Your loving son,

　　　　　　　　　Herbert

Fenton·Ryder
did this.

Seafield House
Bishop Petre School
Wanganui

1 - 4 - 79

Dear Mr. + Mrs. Fenton-Ryder,

Last night I took David under my wing. It appears, from what he told me, that he had been "pushed off" his chair. He had a bruised nose and was suffering from shock. You can rest assured, however, that David will be up and about in no time, and that he will be fine.

He responded well to my mothering, and perked up in no time - a charming lad. Although it took a lot of persuasion to convince him

2.

that medicine was good for him! I hope that he doesn't have to come to me again in the near future. I am sure the chances of his doing so are somewhat remote – he is such a healthy young man.

Yours sincerely,

Prudence Pym
(MATRON)

David Fenton-Ryder. Seafield

SONNET — MY PREP

School   has not anything to show more fair;
Dull would he be of soul who could pass buy
A prep   so touching in its majesty.
  The Page now doth like a garment wear
The beauty of the words, silent, unclear.
  ink, spots, lines curves and letters lie,
Open   unto the world, and to my eye
All bright and glittering in the ~~smokefilled~~ smokeless air
Never did sun most beautifully steep
  in his first splendour valley, rock, or hill,
  Neer saw I, never felt, a calm so deep,!
The   paper resteth at its own sweet will
Dear God! The very words seem asleep
And all that mighty page is lying still.

4 Our Hero progresses through his first year with another letter home which must serve as a preliminary to the inevitable school report and its unavoidable contents revealed to the reader in all its lurid detail; also the happy discovery that Our Hero's once loathed antagonist is again his beloved confederate. A revelation which caused his loving mother some confusion since she had precipitately expressed 'bad feelings' to the mother of Herbert.

Seamreal house
Cwanganui

Dear Mum and Dad, I'm looking forward to
coming home soon and I hope you will like
my report. The exams were all difficult but
I only came bottom in French, Latin and ~~Math~~
Divinity ~~and~~ gas-tube for not coming thaght I did very
well ~~for not coming~~ very bottom in Science, there were
two others that wee worser off than me. Herbert
and I did well in the IIIrd form camp—
we won the prise in two of the games. The
Fergusson and Ginger kept Herbert and me
awake all night, and Chaplain thought it
was me and Herbie, and he fell over our
guy ropes in the dark and broke his pipe,
and he got all hot and excited and blamed
Herbie and me and took away our prises. I
think I heard him (God) swear when he
broke his pipe and I laughed a little and he
wasn't half MAD. My maths wasn't too good
cause I forgot to turn the paper over to see the
questions on the back — had I been told this
I might have come top. Borax had a house
party but me and Herbie had to do all the
washing up cause Borax said me and Herbie
had eaten too much — but he never told us when
to stop. I like history now and my new hero
is Attila the hun, I draw him in art and the
art Master gave me a good mark. I like
the art teacher and the History Master has
got better.
            Love
            David

Say hello to Herc. for me

Bishop Petre School

Report for 1979 **Term,** III

Name FENTON-RYDER. David.   House Sea field.   Form 3. b'

Age 13.9   Average Age of Form 13.8

A C A D E M I C   R E C O R D

SUBJECT	SET	TERM Posn	TERM Ind	EXAM Posn	EXAM %	
English	B'	24/26	D	20/26	36	His improved legibility has revealed a sad deficiency in spelling. P.F.M.
Christian Studies	B'	26/26	E	26/26	14	Must try and take this subject more seriously: David tells me he intends to become a Moslem. A.S.
Social Studies	Hist'	10/26	C	12/26	56	Wrote first class essay on Attila the Hun. J.H.W.
	Geo'	20/26	C	15/26	50	Attitude improved as examinations approached. P.B.D.
Maths.	B'	23/26	D	23/26	17	Good effort made in last week of term J.B
Science	B'	24/26	D	23/26	19	Showed some interest in human Biology. P.McKay.
FRENCH	B'	20/20	C	20/20	30	REFUSES TO BELIEVE PEOPLE ACTUALLY SPEAK THIS LANGUAGE AND THEREFORE IGNORES IT!
LATIN	B'	20/20	E	20/2	3	Cannot remember one word from one day to the next. H.F.S.
PHY ED.	B'	2/26	B	1/26	/	Enjoys his periods very much. B.R.S.
ART	B'	4/26	B	3/26	60	By putting him in a small room by himself he has improved considerably. M.R.W.

Industry Key: A Excellent   B Good   C Average   D Unsatisfactory   E Idle

Cultural and Recreational	**Activity**	
	CHESS	Joined club at beginning of term — have not seen him since. P.W.S.
Awards	/	
School Duties		
Games	**Sport**	
	Hexads.	Much ability but tends to fool around. D.H.H
Awards	/	
Headmaster	Pleased to note that David's industry has improved. Sadly I have had to speak to him too often on the matter of dress and punctuality. He has much potential and needs to recognise this before it is too late. I.D.M.	

Seafield House
Bishop Petre School
Wanganui

END OF YEAR REPORT by Housemaster.

It is very clear from his report that David has not distinguished himself in the classroom this year. I trust that he will return in 1980 determined to approach his studies with greater seriousness and more resolution.

In the House he has tended to be forgetful, untidy, and unruly; and it saddens me to record that he has received more punishments than any other boy of his year. His inventive excuses (recounted with a look of injured innocence) for his misdemeanours have worn a little thin after three terms, a fact which even he is starting to appreciate.

He has made a lively contribution to House Sporting activities, and next year I hope to see him devote his considerable arguing abilities to the House debating team rather than to his friends in the dormitory after lights out !

Despite his troubles he has had a pleasing first year.

Anthony Baipent.

Our Hero discovering a javelin on the
sports field recollects his own intrepid
hero Attila the Hun, and perpetrates
great agitation amongst the onlooking
multitude.

5 Our Hero enters his second year, known confusingly as the Fourth Form. Shedding his puppy fat he starts to look less like a green novice and more like an Old Lag. Gangly and spotty, he moves through this year with all the customary problems and dilemmas associated with those depressed souls who know the world is against them. For Our Hero it is *worse* than having the world and all its fleshy desires agin him, for he has to face single-handedly the bigoted onslaught of the malicious Common Room, and Borax in particular. It is a remarkable feat of superhuman achievement that Our Hero, to put it bluntly, survives.

Our Hero's mother, not realising the immense battle fatigue from which Our Hero has to recover, writes a little note asking why she hasn't heard from him for the first seven weeks of term. Our Hero pens a magnanimous reply in which the reader will observe (both with relief and pleasure) that Our Hero's calligraphy has improved beyond belief, this vast progress having been instigated by the brutal threats of Pug Murphy, the English master, who failed to see the artistic qualities of Our Hero's initial penmanship.

GLENDALE STATION
GORDONSDOWN
New Zealand

Monday.

Dearest Didi,

Not a word from you since you returned to school; you really are rather tiresome. Do hope that this doesn't mean you are into trouble with Borax again — just couldn't stand one of his tedious letters of complaint at the moment.

We really have had one of those weeks. Mary and John came over last Saturday, frightfully worried about young Paul, haven't heard from him since he left London for Turkey, and he has John's Diner's Card. On Sunday, Uncle Peter called in, in a terrible state his best pony has gone lame and the polo tournament is next week.

Met Margo Cranbourne at golf on Monday — said she'd had three letters from Martyn since he'd been back to school, and he'd had four A's and three B's in the last three-weekly order

2

She really can make 2+2 = 10!
Went to Wellington last week to try and buy something to wear on our trip to Tahiti, but not a thing in the shops.
Dad and I both need a break so we're going up to the bach on Sunday, do hope they've got the Spa Pool fixed.
Now Didi, _do_ write!!

Love _Mother._

_P.S._ Having the Guthries to stay from Auckland after we come back from Taupo for the races. They'll want to hear all about you so _please_ write.

_M._

Seafield House

Dear Mum and Dad,
Sorry this letter is late but I've been so busy turning over a new leaf (Borax's idea) and looking after the turds (1st years). The place doesn't change except Borax and Gastube ... who get worse and worse. Herbie thinks Borax is going senile before his time. Me and Herbie were put in charge of the House library on Monday but Borax changed his mind on (~~Tuesday~~) Wednesday cause Hairy Harry the Senior sneak said we were (~~only cutting~~) playing cards - but it wasn't true - we were only cutting cards to see who could borrow a new Educational magazine called Forum.
There's a 1st year turd called (~~Botts~~) Baltimore Jackson whose supposed to be very clever and I help him alot with his maths. Ego Smith says I'm very wise giving Latin up cause he says if I hadn't he would have. I'm going to keep a diary because Herbert says we could be famous one day.
The vomit in the dining hall gets more revulting and I've had to miss several (~~early~~) early morning swims because its made me so sick at nights. Herbie says hes never sure whether hes just eaten his porridge or hes about to eat it a second time. We reckon the eggs come from specially developed chooks which are hard-boiled when they're laid. We managed to stuff two into Gingers mouth the other day without breaking them - we nearly got a third in but he stopped breathing so we pressed his cheeks so he could still function!
I've asked (~~#~~) if I could give up French but Dad told Borax no. Could he change his mind (~~#~~) after all he can't speak French and he does alright.
By the way some turd has pinched my tracksuit so I've brought another one and put it on account. Some one, I've no idea who, I can't even guess, smeared black treacle on Borax's toilet seat, he was flipping wild and threatened to cane the whole house. But I don't see why he's so wild cause he wasn't the first in there - the (~~Ed~~) Chairman of the Board of Governors had supper with him and used it first!
Love, Dave

The 'Treacle'.

6 With an eye to posterity, Our Hero at last decides to keep a diary of the momentous and significant circumstances which daily surround him. Unfortunately, future historians when they consult this invaluable document will find it only spasmodically written.

But to the positive aspect, Our Hero found an old typewriter in the house library. Our Hero also discovered that by using this modern machine (circa 1930) he was able to clear the library of the more boisterous and obstreperous Studious Types.

DIary of ME, david FENTON-Ryder.

Herbert said I ought to keep a diaary so that 1 day when I'm famous I8LL
   be abel to write a auto Biography & get rich.

friDay 13th
         breakfast was as   usual but I won the biggest lump competition which m-
      ade up for it. Frogs eyes, frevnch teacher was in specialy bad mooD
      today & threw a chunk of chalk at me when i asked him how ~~Censored~~
      ~~Censored~~ I was being ~~innocent~~ innocent but Herb
      laughed which made him jump to wrong conclusions..... so mush for edukation.

(CENSORED)

SSaturday   woke up late for breakfast and had cold shower cause I didn't go.
                  i had to tell the prefect I was fainting to get out of the
      shower, otherwisew the brute would have ~~lfte~~ left me in u~~nitl-~~
      ~~untilountil1-~~ until school started. I made a green colour in scienceand
      told Ginger it was lime he drank it but unfortunate y nothing happened. play
      ed hexads all afternoon (& am now firmly convinced that hexads is a
      communist plot to use up all our spare tim e. Old Borax wasnit impressed
      when I told him this.

SUN day   got blasted by headmaster for looking round in chaple prayers,
         but he must of been looking around to see me looking around, thats
      logical. spent the afternoon on a bike ride & almost got lost, did everything
      but wor k.

monDay i HATE mondays. Got woken up at 6 and reminded I had to do my prep.
                  told Herbert i'd already done it & went bak to sleep ....

Pug Murphy gave me another re peat.
      lunch was really awful. I only had bread cause the llook of the other
   stuff put me off. Decided I wanted to do woodwwork so went to see
SHavings about it. He rekoned i'd be good at woodwork and he said that i
         We had an exceptionally exiciting prep. It was a big riot from ~~STfy~~
   start to finish.

<u>tueSDay</u>   ASSembly was borring. HM thought he was speaking to an asssembled m
      mass of 5,000 and raised his voice accordingly. HAIRY Harry has a habit
   of running and jumping itnto bed and we think we'fe cured him cause we
   remobved the matress and when he dived on his bed he nearly smashed every rib

<u>wednesady</u> a normal day.

<u>TH Ursday</u>   spageti for breakfast. Ferguson tipped the whole lot ~~lhot~~* into
   his lap~~all~~ all we could do was laugh so hes trying to get revenge. I'm not
      reallly worried at all.
I made one dollar by cutting Gingers hair, i might start a bussiness, except
   after Gingers haircut I don't think many will come.

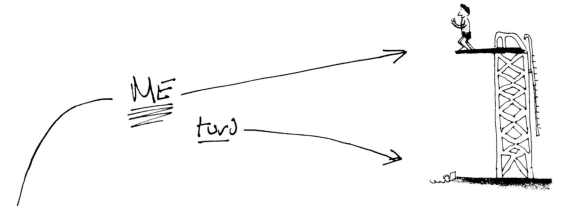

<u>monday</u>   —   SEAFILED House on dining room duties this week. I was
      out the back working the dixhwasher. I accident ly openeded it while it
   '~~saw~~* was going and got wet. wh en my shirt dried it shrank and it hardly
      fits anymore. I also got the prefect wet so I'm on punisyhment.
            I find an~~p~~ apple in my pocket during Christian studies
      and started eating it. God lookked at me as though I had committeed the
   original sin and said cause of insubordiante behaviour he'd give me 2 on
            the tail, so much for the love of god.

<u>Wedn6sday</u> I mumped off the 3 meter diving board for the 1st time and almost
      killed myself. but not nearly as closely as I almost killed one of the
   turds. I missed him by about 2 inchess.

<u>sunDAY</u> I was playing snooker in the afternnoon when I ripped up the table
with the Q. I dònt think Borax will find out cause i glued it
down so well we couldnht notice.

<u>mOnday</u>   rugby began to day at long long last. I AM in the top team for my
age groupp because of my natural ability.

I almost scored a try in the firxst 5 mins, the coach was very
impressed.

<u>tue6day</u>   ;ate for class, told Gastube I was chased by mad dog. not sure that
he believed me.

in woodwork I made a mallett. I discovered tonight that the malleet is
excellent for making sure I'm not disturebed in prep. I don't think
fergusson will flink ink at me again.

<u>wednesda y</u>   we had a house MUSIC practice tead- today. The whole house has
to singa song. Ours id a terrible old fashioned dirge which Borax thinks is
wondefful and goes into rapsody whenever he hears it. I don't know why.
The only exciting bit is when He bert has to sing the highest note.

friDay   the head of Høuse decided that we ought tp have runs. Compulsory.
Apparently it opnes the lungs. I'm not sure why anyone would want his
lungs opneed at that hour of the morning. Any way it gives me pains.

dinner was revolti ng as usual, Herbert found a spider in his potatoe.

HAIRY HARRY THUMPed me today cause I said he was due for a moult.

Hairy Harry

7 In which Our Hero has a slight affray with a new and inexperienced House Tutor. Our Hero and his good friend Herbert are unjustly accused of imbibing gin, when in fact they were doing their best to entertain their battle-weary friends after a hard day at the lodge. The new tutor, fresh from England, totally misunderstood the situation and precipitated Borax into a sudden and obnoxious mood which resulted in ramifications which reached the attention of Our Hero's parents. Our Hero meanwhile continues to do battle with Hexads and the Common Room, and manages a golden duck in house cricket.

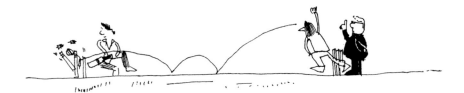

Record — Weekend at the lodge

David Fenton-Ryder

<u>Day One</u> — We set off on our bikes at 1:30
with Mr Pomfrit. It is a long way to bike to the
Lodge and it is raining. Herbert fell off   But I
did <u>Not</u> push him. We arrived at 3:00 and we were
all tired and cold except Mr Pomfret who had
travelled up in a warm car. We cooked our "meal"
(saussiges) and then we had a talk from Mr.
Pomfret about birds. Then we got taken back
because of the misunderstanding. History will correct
this.

Mr Redmond Pomfret...

DOVER COLLEDGE & SHOE PETRE

48

Seafield House
Bishop Petre School
Wanganui

May 2nd, 1980

Dear Mr Fenton-Ryder,

I am afraid I must report to you yet another unfortunate escapade in which David was involved.

Yesterday a small group from the House went up to the Lodge for the weekend on a bird watching expedition. It was a voluntary trip sponsored and led by our newly arrived young House Tutor, Redmond Pomfret, an avid ornothologist.

During the first evening Pomfret noticed David and young Herbert settled in a corner of the room playing cards and sharing a bottle of orange cordial. About an hour later his attention was attracted back to the two boys by David's raucous singing in a very slurred voice a more than indecent version of a popular Chapel hymn. Pomfret immediately went over to David to remonstrate with him and was hit instantly by the fumes of gin coming from the two boys. He immediately suspected the orange drink, picked up their empty bottle and sniffed it. He was left in no doubt. At that moment David turned green, put his head out a nearby window and was violently sick.

Pomfret rang me up, I drove out and brought the boys back to school, a trip punctuated by a number of very unpleasant halts.

I sent the boys straight to bed and saw them this morning when I felt that they would be more in a condition to talk. David admitted he had brought the gin-laced orange drink back to school in his tuckbox. I gave them both six, and as David was the ringleader I gated him for five weeks. I told him further that he had not only let himself down but his House as well. Consequently I would give some thought over the next few days about his representing Seafield in next week's Junior House football match.

I am sorry that once again I must write to you in this vein. Sorry, too, that his gating will co-incide with your planned visit to Wanganui next week for the races. I sincerely hope that the time is not far off when David can curb this precipitate and irresponsible side to his nature.

My regards to both you and Mrs Fenton-Ryder.

Anthony Baird.

Seafield house

Dear Mum,
    Just a brief note to you before Borax writes about a little problem which has arisen.
    We went to the lodge the other day and cause (eat) there's no good water there Herb and I put some orange juice in some old beer bottles and drank it on the first evening. When we had drank it Herb and me started to have some fun by singing a few old world songs. — anyway the new house tutor caught us and said there was gin in the orange, he said we (smell) smelt, but that was only cause Herbie sweats and hadn't washed. Then I was sick cause of the vomit they served for tea and he said I was drunk — well, you know me — that couldn't be true. Anyway, it's all settled — old Borax gave me 6 of the best and it didn't hurt cause I had 4 pairs of underpants on. Herbie yelled a lot.
    Also I had a small problem in a maths test cause I sat next to Ginger who kept showing me his answers. And he got them wrong and I got accused of cheating and of getting them wrong. Nobody's fair here — they're all against me.
    On the (got) good side I've started rowing. Donald (Doc) Duck (master in charge) said I've got the shape now (I've got some hairs on my chest and more under my arms and elsewhere then anybody else in the dorm — apart from Hairy Harry whose due for a moult soon) I've given the piano up to save you the fees and I've volunteered to be confimed by the Bishop (The others bet I wouldn't). My art is still good and would be better if we didn't have a riot everytime we have art lessons
                         Love
                             Dave.

P.S. Cause of the orange juice incident I have been gaited for the weekend — still, hope you can come — £I'm playing house (A) rugby.

8 Our Hero's academic record does not fail to astound all. For Our Reader's perusal, his well known prep on the battle of Agincourt and an obnoxious document called a pink slip. This latter document Our Hero is compelled to carry from class to class in order that the masters may try to keep an eye on Our Hero's dazzling movements.

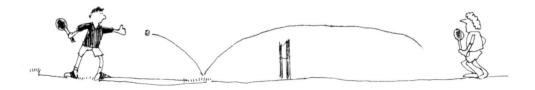

AGINCOURT-

Agincourt was a battle (~~betwen~~) bet ween Henry the fifth and the french. Naturally Henry won. Henry was a strong
's king also he <u>knew</u> how to win battles. The French thought that if they dressed up in plumes and silver armour and flowing robes they would win the war. But the English knew that people who dress up are women so they attacked fearlessly and slaughtered the french. The English were fewer in number but armed with
s X long-bows they slaughtered the French and defeated ~~them~~ They caught them so to
XXX speak with their trousers down in the bog

Their arrows flew so straight and true and were so (~~power full~~) powerful they pun ctured the French armour. The french were so dressed up in armour that they could hardly move. All the English did was bravely rush in and slaughter their horses. (~~Then~~) Then when the knights lay helpless on the ground they decimated them

The main reason the (~~Eg~~) English won was because they
s were brave, <u>corageous</u> and fearless and in short

AGINCOURT.

because they were English also because they had long bows and also because they were (~~fightting~~) fighting the french.
The french always lose to the English
X even at Twickenham. ✓ (C+)

Ferdy Ryder please avoid humour and graphics; I have allowed Mr. Maitel (who comes from France) your French master to ~~read~~ this.

BISHOP PETRE SCHOOL

Report on the work and conduct of ..DAVID FENTON-RYDER..

Date: ..5 JUNE 1980.

Subjects:

1. ENGLISH.   Great oral participation!! P.J.M.
2. — " —.
3. ART   DRAWING SOME FINE CARTOONS
4. Maths   Not naturally gifted.
5. HIST.   Usual patriotic essay against the French!
6. FRENCH   Refuses to enjoy this subject
7. SCI   EXPERIMENT FAILED AGAIN.
8. Acc   Prep late — fell asleep during lesson
9.

9 Miscellaneous documents illustrating the famous life of Our Hero. Our Hero's notes on the famous house debate which won him loud acclaim from the Form and much trouble from the Headmaster; the Matron's snivelling letter home complaining of Our Hero's hygiene, and finally, yet another odious document from his Housemaster.

M.C. L+G : Two headmasters not better than one. The One we got at moment bad enough imagine it in doses of two! Two assemblies a week! - You would not just get 6 of the best - You get 12! That = sore bum. Fees would go up X2 and parents would get 2 nasty rude letters instead of usual one. Everything be twice as bad as before. The Board would have to build ANOTHER big house. Anyway everyone hates headmaster so silly to get two.

Debating Notes from Our Hero, 1980

Seafield House
Bishop Petre School
Wanganui

6 - 6 - 80

Dear Mrs. Fenton-Ryder,

I am writing this note to seek your co-operation over problems I am having with David. I am sorry to say that he tends to be rather grubby— unwashed hair, dirty knees and teeth often unbrushed. The other day I made him open his drawers and I took out five pairs of underpants, two singlets and three football socks all unwashed; not to mention an assortment of stale biscuits, sticky toffees and bad apples.

I really think that David should think more responsibly about his general cleanliness and tidiness, and I would be most appreciative if you wrote him a note supporting me over this matter.

In other ways David is a delightful young man, and so often most helpful. Only the other evening he offered to wash up after a small sherry party I had before the staff dinner.

I hope both you and Mr. Fenton-Ryder are well.

Yours sincerely,
Prudence Pym.

Portrait of our much-loved Matron in her delightfully modern attire, with her dog, which Our Hero once managed to lose on the golf course.

Seafield House
Bishop Petre School
Wanganui

HOUSEMASTER'S REPORT

David's School report in no way suggests that he has laid
sound foundations for his School Certificate chances in
'81. Industry ratings and exam marks are both disappointing.

A succession of incidents over the year has not made life
easy for me or any of my officials. "The new leaves" which
he insistently assured me, on so many occasions, that he
intended to turn over could be bound into a sizeable volume.

I commend him for his contribution to House debating and
rugby, and trust these positive endeavours will widen into
other areas next year.

Anthony Baffert.

10 Our Hero enters the Fifth Form, a critical year with the horizon darkened by School Certificate and other trivial hurdles which must be circumnavigated. Our Hero discovers he is a man (Ecce Homo) and writes his first letter of love. Fortunately, this letter survives for our edification since Herbert copied it for the general interest of all in the Dormitory and elsewhere. The Reader is indeed most fortunate in so far as this account of Our Hero's life is supported by parts of an accompanying diary composed by a young English Tutor who considered himself most fortunate to be an onlooker at some of Our Hero's great escapades. This chapter includes a sea-battle in which Our Hero succeeds in sinking the 1st VIII boat, and contrives to turn a harmless game of cricket into a battle royale equal only to Agincourt and Crécy on the same field. We also share some of the views of his father.

Dear Daphne,
I hope all is going well with you and
I did enjoy the walk out during half term !!!!!
you managed Hope you weren't too late home and
woolly. to get all that straw out of your

Herbie, Cheryl's boyfriend, is going
to have a party at his house in Wellington.
We're going to have a real fun do — don't worry
about the adults cause Herbie's parents will be
in the South Island.
Don't forget... you are the light of my
Life, Spangle of my heaven, Horizon of all my Desires,

Yours truely,

Darling Dave. xxx

P.S. Have you got my bike pump.

Rowing

All the way upstream David Fenton-Ryder found it difficult to concentrate on the job in hand since he found great interest in various flotsam and scenes on the bank. Eventually he had been persuaded to pay attention by the coach whose temper was running short.

However, on the return journey David's sharp eyes caught sight of a young couple amongst the willows and he was unable to contain his curiosity. The coach, meanwhile was becoming concerned about an approaching corner and his driver's apparent lack of knowledge about it. With the merest glance over his shoulder he bellowed David's name. At this point things happened very quickly, which is surprising for Fenton-Ryder; in his panic he whirled around grabbing for the control stick on the outboard which caused not only his sun hat to fall over his eyes, but also the control stick to come towards him and the throttle to open.

The coach was suitably pleased with the reaction to his outburst and allowed himself a faint smile as he turned away. The smile then froze on his lips as he saw with horror the impending disaster.

THE FIRST EIGHT ROWING COACH

February 1981

Dear Mr Fenton-Ryder,

I regret to inform you that your son was involved nay caused, severe damage to a coach boat and the sinking of the first's practice boat.

As you will know, we agreed to accept David as a coach boat driver to help in the training of our various rowing teams. Due to unfortunate circumstances I was forced to ask David to come with me on this particular day.

Throughout the trip I had to keep reminding him of the job in hand for he found it difficult to keep his eyes from wandering. On this particular occasion we were in danger of climbing a twenty foot bank, and crossing a paddock. As perceived, your son had found something of particular interest on the bank that we had passed.

I rapidly caught his attention and brought him back to reality. At this particular point I feel he lost his presence of mind for he opened the throttle on the outboard motor and steered directly towards the eight.

I will not bore you with a detailed description of the damage which occured. However, I must inform you that at least part of the cost of repairs will have to be met by yourself. I have also banned him from the river.

Yours sincerely,

Redwan Pomfret.

St. Agnes.
Sunday.

Dearest David,

I will be happy to join you for the party in Wellington. It wasn't easy since daddy was angry with being so late back last time. I've got to bring ~~Cheryl~~ Trish and Fiona – it was the only way daddy would let me go. Fiona said she saw you out with one of those beastly High School girls, but I said that couldn't be right, could it?? That reminds me – I haven't got your bike pump, so where did you leave it??

Lots of love,

Your Daph.
xxx

Cricket

A lovely summer's afternoon one Saturday in March. The air was filled with the heavy sounds of cricket: the frenzied unintelligible shout often related to How's That, the click of willow against leather and slap of flesh from an admiring crowd of onlookers.

The match we are particularly interested in is the 7th XI who are pitting their talent, energy and wits against the much-feared team from St Fieldmouse on the Hill. The indomitable Fenton-Ryder has been selected to represent the school in this all-important game. St Fieldmouse is now batting, chasing the effort of OUR TEAM. The tension is high in the field as every run counts, and Fenton-Ryder is right there in the close field, leaping uncharacteristically on anything that moves — including the batsman at times.

On this particular occasion the ball, having struck the bat, rolls down the pitch. Everybody lurches into action as the batsmen scurry down the wicket while the fieldsmen try to recover the ball, but no one is as desperate as Fenton-Ryder who drives headlong across the wicket, arms outstretched for the ball, but over the batsman's feet. In a flash the two opponents are facing each other: Fenton-Ryder with anger written all over his face, the other with indignation. The inevitable occurs.

7th XI Cricket Coach.

<u>MEMO TO:</u>   Seafield House

Is nothing Fenton-Ryder-proof?

This doesn't seem possible, but I had a full scale brawl during my cricket match on Saturday.   Then again, anything's possible with that idiot.

One week he's thrown off the river because he sinks a boat and damages another, and the next week he reduces a perfectly normal cricket match to a back-street brawl.

Until then he had been fielding quite well. Jumping left, right and centre to stop the balls and then next minute he runs half-way across the pitch and dives headlong across the path of one of the batsman to pick up a ball.   Well, naturally the poor batsman couldn't get out of the way and fell flat on his face.   The next second, these two are laying into each other while the rest join in.   Why nobody got hurt seriously when there were bats, stumps, bails, balls and God knows what flying around, I'll never know.

What I want to know now is what on earth do we do with him?

P.S.   Do you know if he's coming back next year?

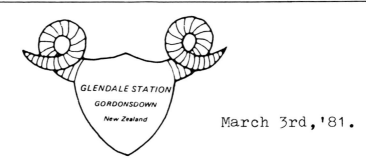

GLENDALE STATION
GORDONSDOWN
New Zealand

March 3rd,'81.

My Dear Boy,

What the devil's going on? We have just had a letter
from your housemaster with his usual unpleasant comments
about your behaviour, and enclosing two reports from
other masters.

The first report was from that young fellow Pomfret,
whom you fell foul of last year at the Lodge, claiming
that you had just about written off all the School
Rowing Club plant. The second was from a bloke, whose
name I couldn't read, stating that you had turned a
cricket match into some sort of version of "On the Mat".

Now, allowing for the usual schoolmaster's exaggeration
it would seem that you've made an ass of yourself. Also,
you have involved me in the river incident, as it is
suggested that I meet the cost of part of the damage!
I want a letter back from you pronto telling me exactly
what happened. I'm not made of money, you know, and I'm
not paying up until I get all the facts.

The whole unpleasant business has upset your Mother,
particularly as the first inkling she had of it was from
Margo Cranbourne, who came out with some outrageous
version of the story in front of us all - in the Members'
Stand bar on Saturday! Doubtless, she got it all from
that little squirt, Martyn.

Now, get cracking and let me know what happened.

Your Mother sends her love. She's out at golf and I'm
just off to the Club.

Father

11

In which Our Hero totally justifies his epic actions to his father and tries to shift the emphasis of his Dear Father's concerns elsewhere.

Appendix to this chapter: an odious document, discovered in the Common Room, that suggests Our Hero is incompetent in matters relating to such trivia as public examinations.

Seafield House

Dear Father,
Thank-you for your letter. Sorry about the small bill you have recieved. Actually I was lucky to get away with my life, Pomme Fritter could have killed me. I was trying to steer clear of some timber and Pommefritter insisted I opened up the throttle just as the 1st 8 slowed down and the next thing I knew I'd cut their boat in half, and I bravely helped pick them all up. It shouldnt be too espensive since the boat was more than 2 years old.

As for the Cricket match that was nothing to do with me and the rest of the team are prepared to write and tell you the same : the other team started it and got all they deserved. Anyway cricket's finished and I'm Captain of the House Rugby Team. Borax is getting better with me now cause he wants to win the cup, last year, they say, when we lost he broke down and cried on the sideline. The Headmaster's got a new car so I expect the fees will go up neat term. Herbert's invited me down to Wellington for the 1st week of the holiday — hope this is okay — we want to study our English and Maths together so School Cert. goes well. You'll be pleased to know I'm going on a D of E tramp next term.

Love, Dave

P.S. - We got ticked off by God because we (got) gave so little in the collection. On Wednesday he came into class with a new suit on !!!
P.P.S. The boat I sunk was only an Italian one ;— It must be cheap.

BISHOP PETRE SCHOOL

INTERIM REPORT AND ASSESSMENT FOR SCHOOL CERT. CANDIDATES

NAME....FENTON-RYDER , DAVID....HOUSE.SEAFIELD...FORM.5B.

ENGLISH If 25% ~~was~~/were the pass mark, he would still fail.

MATHEMATICS It would seem his chances at English are better than Maths.

ART Rate his chances highly but higher still if we could enter his graffiti.

HISTORY —Yes— if he remembers his historical dates as well as his St. Agnes dates.

SCIENCE If it is rated more on the Human Biology side.

FRENCH If he posses this it will be as much a surprise to me as to learn that Attila, the Hun, had taken up embroidery.

12 In which Our Hero is the root cause of an ongoing mystery comparable to the Quest for the Holy Grail and as insoluble as any Sherlock Holmes case. He achieves National Fame by appearing in the local newspaper, being broadcast over the radio and sought by the police, but although examined by the keenest minds in the Common Room's Inquisition Torture Chamber reveals nothing. Our Reader, however, has a few valuable insights through some personal correspondence which has only just come to light.

Radio Announcement

Mystery still shrouds the disappearance of five boys on an expedition from Bishop Petre School. The five failed to turn up at the second of their two campsites after what should have been a fairly easy day's walking along roads and tracks across farmland and through some dense bush. School authorities are mystified as to how or where the party could have become lost, especially considering the excellent weather conditions. However, they are not unduly worried, since the boys are well-equipped with tents, maps and food. A search is now in progress.

CUTTING FROM LOCAL NEWSPAPER
TWO DAYS LATER . . .

BOYS FOUND — MYSTERY STILL UNSOLVED

The five boys who have been missing in the bush have suddenly reappeared, but the mystery surrounding their disappearance remains unsolved.

The boys, all from BISHOP PETRE SCHOOL, were taking part in an expedition for the Bronze Award of the Duke of Edinburgh Scheme when they disappeared. They failed to turn up at the second of their two campsites on Tuesday evening.

School authorities are totally mystified as to just how and where they became lost.

"All they had to do was follow the road or tracks."

However, the master in charge was not worried.

"They all have their own equipment which includes food, tents, maps and compasses," said Mr Pomton-Fritte.

The boys, all aged 15-16, seemed no worse for their ordeal. They appeared at the campsite two days later having evaded all efforts to find them.

One of the boys, David Fenton-Ryder said "The maps provided by the school were faulty and we took a wrong turn."

However, Mr Pom-Fritter, who has recently joined the staff, was not convinced, but added optimistically, "It shouldn't take too long to find out what actually happened."

Nevertheless, to date, the mystery remains unsolved, and Senior-Sergeant Bishop of the local S.A.R. could shed no light on the matter.

"It's nothing to do with us now."

Young David Fenton-Ryder, the spokesman for the group was equally non-committal.

"It's a long story!"

Mr Pompous-Fretton said the boys would be closely questioned once back in school.

Seafield House,
Bishop Petre School.

Dear Mother and Father,

You probably know by now about David's bad behaviour on the Duke of Edinburgh tramp, so I thought I'd better tell you the whole story. We had to tramp through air crash gully and beyond. David decided to go and see this girl from St. Agnes who lives nearby. We got lost and I had to spend the night on a damp floor and I got a cold. Pomp-frit got very mad and David can't do D. of E. again — he took all the blame and so he should have done. All the facts aren't out yet but I'll tell you later if I can remember. Could I buy another track suit please I lost them on the tramp with my boots and raingear.

Love to all,
Herbert.

P.S. David sends his love.

Dear Daph,

Don't say anything about our visit - they still think we all got lost! Did you see it in the local rag - they say it was on the radio.

I think the Headmaster's guessed even though we fooled silly PommeFritter. In fact the Head's flipping wild but we've managed to stick to our story. Herbert's worried sick but can't do anything cause I said I'd drop him in it over the smoking racket. Did your dad ever find out we all slept in the shearer's quarters?

Now the dust's settled down the other lads see I'm a natural leader. I might get a game with the 2nd <u>XV</u> next week. I've stopped smoking cigs now I've found a pipe better.

Farewell, light of my life,

Love   Dave.

P.S. Eat this letter when you've finished it's red-hot (like my new pipe!)

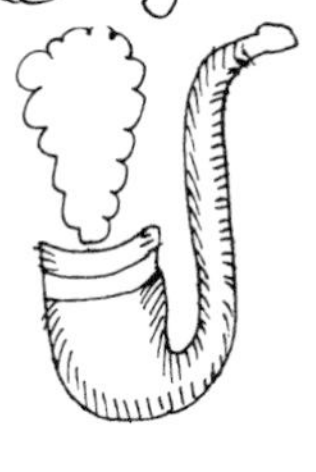

13 In which the School at long last recognises the academic genius of Our Hero when the Housemaster, with a mere miserable postcard, announces that School Certificate was passed . . . if not with distinction, at least with dignity. A letter from Our Hero rightly complaining about the conditions under which he is forced to live, and leaving us with utter admiration at his determination in being prepared to sustain yet further years in what he himself described as the only lunatic asylum run entirely by the inmates.

SCHOOL CERTIFICATE RESULTS

candidate no. 307 065 27 Fenton Ryder David.

SUBJECT	MARK	GRADE
ART	80%	A
HISTORY	70%	A
ENGLISH	60%	B
MATHS	50%	B
SCIENCE	50%	C
FRENCH	40%	C
		NA.

Seafield
Jan 23rd.

Dear David,
    Your S.C. marks to hand.
Five passes and 80% in Art,
well done! Must say H.M.
and I gasped when we realised
you had elevated yourself to
the exalted heights of the 6th.

    We expect hard work this
year, especially as your two
study companions, Herbert
Smith and "Ginger" Cranborne
may be going into 7D.
Regards to your parents,

Anthony Bassent

Commonwealth Day
14 March 1983
New Zealand
24c

Mr David Fenton-Ryder
Glendale Station
Gordonsdown.

Seafield House

Dear Mum and Dad,
　　It really is a waste of my time and your well earnt money keeping me in this prison camp. Having had such an excellent time in the holiday I realise how much I'm missing out on life.
　　Borax, Gastube, Sparrow, even God are hell-bent on making my life a misery. This place is too horrible to describe, I can see it all now I'm a sixth former. You've no idea how I suffer. They treat us like small kids and other times its worse than a Syberian prison camp. Anyway, that little jerk Martyn Cranbourne (Ginger is too good a name for him) and Herbert have gone straight into the 7th form - 7D is full of big-headed swots who spend all their available time creeping about the masters.
　　Anyway, who wants to be a blueshirt. Matthew left last year and he's doing okay, he's got a job at a local kiwi fruit place and has his own car and says he's getting engaged soon.
　　Every one seems pretty shocked at me getting school cert, Gas tube said he was going to demand a recant, but I think he was kidding. Someone said he lost $5:00 with another science master we call the Barcelona Nun over my results. Everytime I see a master in the Common Room they keep looking at me with blank amazement, and God clasps his hands together and looks at the sky. I think he's joking but you cant be sure with him. I don't see why they're all surprised - School Cert. was easy — anyway they're all trying to take the credit, but it was me who did all that last-minute work.
　　　　　　　　Love.
　　　　　　　　　　Dave

P.S. If I get U.E. This year can I please leave?

14 Contains a letter in which Our Hero clearly demonstrates the detention atmosphere of the School, and his determined effort to withstand the puritanic backlashes of the Housemaster. This chapter also contains an affectionate and matronly-type letter from his mother as well as a nauseating and offensive letter from Martyn Cranbourne's whining and vain mother who whimpers and snivels about her son's association with Our Hero.

Dear Mum and Dad,
I've got the study fixed now, Martyn Cranbourne did nothing and moans all the time cause hes in the same study as Fergusson and me. Even Herberts fed up with him now he's got over the first flush of thinking he's Gods gift to potential scholarship. I don't think Herberts going to make the 7th form – he's fed up with all the work and he isn't a natural creep like the rest. I put those Penthouse posters up, but Borax took them all down, though we noticed that he carefully folded them and took them away under his arm. Because Herbert and I like pickled onions the other two keep complaining about the smell.

Fergusson tried a counter attack with smelly socks but Martyn Cranbourne just moans and snivels all the time. We tried to ~~Martyn~~ teach Martyn a lesson the other day by connecting the mains to the door handle, but Borax used it first, it blew a fuse in the House but not such a fuse as Borax blew!

We've got No 5 study (the ratbag one) with the smoking cellar right beneath the carpet. I've given up smoking now but Herbert still likes the occasional cigar and Fergusson uses that large Swiss pipe. Borax came into the study the other day when they were down in the cellar, we didn't have time to put the floor-boards back, but we covered the hole with the carpet. When he got to the door he asked if Herbert and Fergusson would come and see him when they arrived back and looked straight at the carpet – I reckon he knew all the time. He also picked up Herberts dictionary which has the inside cut out to hide his cigars – fortunately it was empty: the last one was in Herberts mouth under the carpet. I reckon someone squealed.

2

You know we collect beer cans and decorate the room with them - Borax just happened to pick up two steineys which were full - that was Herberts fault - he forgot to empty them down the drain. I (~~dad~~) think its funny he knew all this - I (~~still~~) dont think he's (~~mad~~) got a sixth sense - I reckon Martyn Cranbourne squealed.

Love Dave

P.S. Have just heard that Herbs coming back into the sixth. Borax thinks the work is too hard but Herb says he's missing the good time!

Behind the old factory.

'Ginger' (Martin)
Cranbowrne.

GLENDALE STATION
GORDONSDOWN
New Zealand

Sunday.

Dearest Didi,

Do hope things are working out better in the study – Quite certain that you and Herbert will make it up. All he could have in common with that little twerp Martyn is that they are both in 7D! They've probably got a lot to talk about over school work at the start of the year and that's why you feel left out.

That dreadful Margo Cranbourne keeps shouting everywhere about how the school "begged them to let Martyn go into the 7th" You could hear her half way across the golf course last Friday! (Can't imagine where the child got his brains from – Margo even failed School Certificate Home Economics, and Dad says Rupert was as thick as a brick at school.)

Glad the stereo's going well, and Dad says you can buy a new chair for the study, and charge it up – too much of a fag bringing one down from the bach.

Do you mean to say that all Martyn contributed to the study was an old worn-out kettle from the Shearers' quarters.!"

Bring Herbert out to dinner with you if you like, when we come over next week.

Dad's flat out with the races coming up, as three of the stewards are overseas.

We'll have a good chat next week.

Love,
Mother.

Wessex Hills Station
Gordonsdown

February 16th, 1982

Dear Mr Baigent,

Rupert and I are very concerned about
Martyn's study companions. We are, naturally,
embarrassed to bring the matter up, and we
certainly do not want to appear complaining
parents. But we are most anxious that Martyn
does both himself and the School credit
academically this year, and we feel that
this will be made difficult for him if he
remains in the same study as David Fenton-
Ryder.

Please understand, we have nothing against
David as a boy, but he does not take school-
work very seriously, and from all accounts
has got himself into rather a lot of trouble
at school over the years. The boy is not
entirely to blame, as he has been terribly
spoilt at home, and really runs quite wild in
the holidays.

We know little about the other boy,
Herbert Smith, but we believe he is a close
friend of David's, and that disturbs us.

When the Headmaster wrote to us suggesting
that Martyn go into 7D he said that he felt
sure that Martyn would have a splendid year.
We are most anxious that he does, but feel this
could be jeopardised by his being in Number 4
study.

We are quite confident that Martyn
could never be led astray or do anything
unworthy of his family or his House,
but we would like to see him go through the
year with as few disturbing distractions as
possible.

We do hope you can give some thought
to this problem. This letter has been written

Margo
Cranbourne.

out of concern for Martyn only, and in no
way is intended as a criticism of your
study arrangements.

When we saw you at the start of term
we were quite serious in the offer of our
bach in the May holidays, should you and Mrs
Baigent like a week in Taupo - we never use
it during the duck-shooting season.

Yours sincerely,

Margo Cranbourne

15 Our Hero's close ally makes contact with the dead and is only saved by Our Hero's immediate attention. Martyn Cranbourne suffers certain indignities brought about by some ancient rites, and Borax and God become more sensible.

Seafield House
Bishop Petre School
Wanganui

Since I will not be able to be present at the meeting concerning the conduct of Herbert Smith here is a written statement of my findings.

As you know I came across a strange gathering of boys the other evening through a loud, muffled exclamation, from one of the studies. On investigation there were no lights burning in any of the studies and no other noises. Perceiving something may be wrong I decided to reconnoitre the situation from a window.

Being a back study, I had diffulty reaching the desired window, but was rewarded by the fact that there were no outside lights to reveal my person, the window was open and the curtains were only partially closed.

The situation inside was similar to what I had always imagined as a séance: the three boys in question were seated around a circular board with a glass in the middle. The room was in total darkness so it took me sometime to adjust.

I have no idea how long they had been there but I was certainly there for about ten minutes and witnessed various black magic rituals like reading the Lord's Prayer backwards. I also know my name occurred at various times, but I was amply rewarded when on turning on a desk lamp below the window my face was illuminated which caused Herbert to faint while the others stared blankly for several moments before the curtains were violently closed.

What happened next is still rather a blurr. I heard exclamations and quite a large amount of movement. This I thought was the best moment to act. Unfortunately, the window **was** not easy to gain access **through** and having finally reached the inside I was struck on the head by something and in the consequential disorientation I then became entangled in the curtain.

On emergence the boys had disappeared plus the various artifacts.

Redman Pomfret.

Seafield House

Dear Mum and Dad,
    Things are getting serious here. It all started as a joke then things went wrong. We decided to have a seance and get into some black magic. Well it started off funny enough - Herbert made a wax effigy of Martyn Cranbourne and (he) we stuck some cocktail sticks on it. In the middle of the seance the Matrons cat came into the study and brushed against Herbs leg. Herb started and the cat ran out. Herbert refused to beleive it was the cat and said he had been touched by the spirits of the Dead! I laughed and laughed but the next day Martyn Cranbourne got a boil on his bum just where we had been sticking the cocktail sticks in the effigy. Next thing I know, Herb's off to (faith) Faith Healing services in some weird church set up and taking it all seriously. He thought the world was going to end and that Satan would appear - he thought the number 666 was special.
    The Chaplain said he got it from the book of Revelation in the Bible and he said the Book of Revelation was the happy hunting ground of all cranks. Anyway, to cut a long story short, The Chaplain and Borax took me seriously and I think they've sorted Herbert out - at least I hope they have - Herbert's my best friend and its worried me sick seeing him turning into a freak. To be fair to God and Borax they seem to be getting better, they understand the situation and us better these days
                                    Love
                                    Dave

P.S. { I've decided to really get stuck into Rugby - Mr. Baigent is keen our house does well. }

Strange encounters with a cat leading Herbert into the belief that he has made contact with the dead.

Séance . . . from the Oxford Dictionary . . . sitting of a society or deliberative body; meeting for exhibition or investigation of spiritualistic phenomena. (F, f.l. *sedere* — to sit.)

16 Our Hero becomes the unfortunate victim of Circumstances Beyond His Control. Falling into the hands of wicked and trendy men he only escapes by the gallant efforts of himself.

Rodney: our trendy social worker.

Darling Daph,

Don't listen to those silly rumours about me, this letter will give it to you straight from the horses mouth. We all had to go to one social project or another for the sixth form activity week, and I chose to go to Wellington for a week to work in the Down and Out's centre. When Pom-frit discovered he had to go, as well he decided Heb would go elsewhere, to split us! As soon as we got to Wellington, Pom-frit leaves me with this social worker, who speaks with a slight lisp and called me 'Didi' as Mum does. He (was) seemed a bit of a joke but was good at buying me the occasional beer and didn't mind me smoking my pipe. On the Thursday evening you mentioned in your letter, this social worker called Rodney took me to his favorite pub — I thought it was a bit "queer" — that is literally !! Cause when I got in there, there wasn't a single girl or woman in (place) sight. I twigged it was a gay bar, God did I feel my face going red! I didn't know where to put myself — then the Police Raid started, so I thought "Fenton-Ryder, if you get caught in a gay bar you'll never be able to return to Seafield"

I didn't think — I just reacted — I dived into the bogs, dodgy I grant you — once in there, I climbed through the window, out along a ledge. For the sake of (my) my reputation anything had to do- so I climbed in another window — down a corridor full of low glowing red lights and burst out into the street straight into the arms of Pom-frit, who had the nerve to ask what was I doing coming out of a massage parlour. Better than a gay bar I said and he thought

I meant he was gay and got wild What I'd like to know: what was he doing outside a massage parlour in the first place. As usual I was the unfortunate victim of circumstances beyond my control — that's the truth — so ignore the rumours. See you at the dance,

Lots of Love
Dave

P.S. They locked Rodney up !!!!

<u>Tuesd</u>. I was compulsorarily voluntdeered for the choir. I sang out of tune
during rehearsals to get out but it only made old fish the music master say   I
was an alto so I'm singing with the turds.. it snot fair.

<u>Wednesday</u>T.___ during art I disvcovered the way to become famous is to splatter
paint on the paper and then call it a 'psychovisual experience' or an ab-
stract representation of a happy onion (thyre both the same thing(. The
art teacher prohihits such work because he says it will lead too mus mass
riots, but really its because hes deeply puritanic and he thinks free
expression ruins the soul. What rot.

<u>SUnday.</u> Read lexson in chapel read Acts chapter 2 and forgot to turn page of
Bible ovee and so finished with the statement that the apostles were
drunk. god was furious, I should have finisyed with statement that they were
filled with the Holy spirit. lucky god isnt a charismatic otherwise he'd
have sent me to hell....if he could.

<u>Monday</u>___ had argument whether Borax had sense of humour, i said he did and the
others asked me to prove it. So i put all the desks against the door
and all we could see was the top of his baldheead bouncing up and down to look
over to see what was happening. Unfortunately he didnt have a sense of
humour.

<u>tuesday</u> the school choir is going to sing Jerusalem again at parents weekend, itsd
the HM's favourite hymn and we al, wish he'd forget it. Herbert reckons the
'satsnic mills' have something-too- to do with the studios in the headmasters
mind. God88's favourite hymn is cum rondda, we sing it every day in
chapel and i reckon the ,'I am weak but thou art mighty' does wonders for
his ego.

<u>RThursday</u> For sujmmer sport I put down for official Tennis but since Skippy's
in charge both of tennis and debating it doesnt matter if I don't turn
up aso long as he thinks I8m preparing for debates.

<u>Frid.</u> Firedrills in house...big riot. Fergussion's young brother ju mped out
t of the wrong upstairs window and it was the wrong one ,... .he was
left hanging onto window sill by his finger tips and it took 3 people to pu,ll
-yhim back in. One of the turds was so confused he got half dressed and came
out to report area half ready for school and half ready for bed.

<u>Sat.</u> Herb had birthday today and we threw him into pond by golf course withall
his clothes on. He almost pulled me in with him, but I have forgiven him bec
ause his parents sent him a aparcel of food which he left unattended in his
study. It was nice food too.

Report to HEADMASTER of 4th Year Activity Week

As pre-arranged, I accompanied half-a-dozen boys to various social welfare institutions in Wellington. The boys were split between various organisations and worked well and hard under some extraordinary pressures throughout the week.

Therefore it is with some regret that I must inform you of one particular incident which occurred on Thursday evening.

I was relaxing in my hotel room when I was disturbed by a loud commotion in the street. On investigation I perceived a crowd gathering around the entrance to a building a little way down the street. From whence a group of policemen were apprehending various persons. My attention was then drawn to a couple of our boys standing nearby.

Concerned for the boys spectating I quickly joined them in order to tell them to move away in case they were deemed suspicious by the police. The boys duly dispersed while I tried to ascertain exactly what had warranted the police action.

At that moment Fenton-Ryder emerged from the entrance I was standing by quite uncontrollably, thus failing in any attempt to avoid my person. Which he consequentially collided with at high speed. However, the main cause for complaint was due to the fact that not only had he just emerged from a downtown "massage parlour" (which can only be regarded as disreputable), but also implied in his reply to my inquiry of his actions that I was someway involved in or with a "gay bar".

In his defence later Fenton-Ryder claimed the social worker whom **he** had been accompanying had taken him to the "bar". This I can now support since on further investigation I discovered that the social worker in question was being held by the police. It also appears that Fenton-Ryder, in his efforts to escape the "bar" and police raid, had entered the "massage parlour" unknowingly. However, what is impossible to ascertain is whether or not he entered the "bar" under the impression it was part of his work.

Therefore I must conclude that Fenton-Ryder was perhaps not in control of all the facts in the situation and any punishment should be considered in this light.

Redman Pomfret.

Seafield House
Bishop Petre School
Wanganui

October 24th, 1982.

Dear Mr Fenton-Ryder,

I need not go over the unfortunate incident in which David was involved down in Wellington last week. The Headmaster has written to you and given you all the facts.

My purpose in writing is to assure you that in no way was David to blame, and, indeed, I commend him for his presence of mind and initiative in avoiding what could have been a very nasty and unsavoury affair for both him and the school.

Confidentially I have never been happy about the boys being let loose around the country, and handed over to people about whom we know very little. More particularly when we put them under the care of "do gooders" who talk in sociological clichés, belong to every trendy protest movement, and generally have absolutely no sense of occasion. I am sure this recent lesson will make us more selective in future.

I have made it quite clear to David that I hold him in no way responsible for what happened. I am pleased to say he looks back on the affair with sensible good humour.

My regards to Mrs Fenton-Ryder.

Yours sincerely,

Anthony Baipent.

17

Which contains the record of a dialogue between the House-master and the House Matron in which at long last Our Hero is seen in the right light. Our Hero returning with his associate, Herbert, victorious from a Schools' Debating competition, finds the house in total havoc, and succeeds in rescuing the House Matron, quelling a mutiny, putting Martyn Cranbourne down irrevocably, and leaving the House Tutor in a bad light; the sum total being that whereas everybody else was covered in ink, Our Hero is covered in glory. The readers will be grateful for the record of this conversation given in full by Herbert who gained a cold in the ear from listening at a draughty keyhole.

The Dialogue

Housemaster: Good morning, Matron

Matron: It may be good this morning, but it wasn't last night!

Housemaster: Ah, yes! What actually happened?

Matron: That wretched boy Cranbourne!!

Housemaster: Dear oh dear — he was a contender for next year's Head of House. You sure it was Cranbourne?

Matron: He was the main instigator, as he always is, in his sly hypocritical way!

Housemaster: Do sit down and tell me what happened. Tea?

Matron: Yes please, cream and just 3 sugars, please.

Housemaster: What exactly did Cranbourne do?

Matron: Well, I was enjoying a coffee with *dear* Mr Offenbach when it started. I went to the study area and there was ink everywhere — and when I opened the door that *wretched* boy Cranborne squirted ink all over my new dress!

Housemaster: Who was the tutor? I know the prefects were with the Headmaster.

Matron: Oh that *silly* young man had gone to the video room to watch a birdwatching film with some first years. There was a dreadful row, until David walked in.

Housemaster: David?

Matron: David Fenton-Ryder.

Housemaster: Oh, no — I'm beginning to see the problem.

Matron: No, I don't think you are, Mr Baigent. David saved the situation.

Housemaster: Fenton-Ryder?

Matron: Yes, he stopped that awful Cranbourne boy, and when David appeared the others retreated like scolded puppies.

Housemaster: I'd have thought Fenton-Ryder would have been up to his eyebrows in such a riot!

Matron: Certainly not! He and Herbert had just arrived back from the school debating — victorious, I might add — and he took total control.

Housemaster: I don't know what to think.

[*Editor's Note: gap here because Herbert had to leave the keyhole for fear of sniggering.*]

Matron: . . . there's no doubt David would make a good Head of House.

Housemaster: Set a thief to catch a thief as they say.

Seafield House
Bishop Petre School

Dear Rodney,
                I've been told to write and thank you
for a 'lovely' week. It was supposed to make
me aware of another side of life - the down
and outs.
        And the stay certainly made me aware of a
type of person I hadn't "experienced" before,
you showed me the lesser known spots of
Wellington - which was most educational as they
were places I would never have been to by
myself.
        Apart from one rough spot I had a
"gorgeous" time, thanks to you.

        Thank-you once again.

        Yours Sincerely

                David Fenton-Ryder

P.S.   When will they let you out of jail ??

18 In which Our Hero aspires to the Seventh Form as Head of Seafield House. A justifiable decision in the eyes of our readers, a calculated risk in the reckoning of the Headmaster, and a major error according to Martyn Cranbourne's mother. These considerations are aptly illustrated by a note from the Headmaster to the Housemaster, yet another snivelling letter from Margo Cranbourne anxious about the social ramifications of Our Hero's aggrandizement, and a letter from Our Hero's fag showing that the Reformation was not a once-only event.

MEMO TO: A.T.B. Seafield House

Dear Tony,

I thought I'd write to you about that young man Fenton-Ryder. Despite what I have said to you earlier, I think that perhaps your "gamble" has somehow worked.

Today he approached me about the initiation ceremonies I mentioned in assembly. He told me quite frankly, that by warning the School of the degrading nature of these ceremonies, I was undermining School spirit.

Of course, he is quite wrong, but still his affection for School tradition is to be greatly admired. He must, however, get his hair cut. Once this has been done, he will be a fine all-round Man.

Wessex Hills Station
Gordonsdown

February 27th, 1983.

Dear Mr Baigent,

Rupert and I are very unhappy about
Martyn's role in Seafield this year.

Your decision to appoint David Fenton-
Ryder as Head of House is, of course, your
affair. I can only say, however, that it
has raised a few eyebrows. But for Martyn
to hold only a minor position of authority
has come as a great shock to him and us.

I rather feel that you have not appreciated the fact that Martyn responds extreme-
ly well to encouragement and responsibility -
at the moment, it would seem, he is receiving
neither. It appears that Martyn is being
held entirely responsible for that silly
little ink-throwing incident at the end of
last year, and he is being made to suffer
for the rest of his time at Seafield.

I am not by nature a complaining parent,
but I must raise my voice in protest against
what I believe is an injustice. Rupert and I
would have come over this week-end to raise
the matter with you personally, but unfortunately Rupert has had a bad attack of asthma.

I do hope you will give the matters
raised in this note sympathetic consideration.

Sincerely,

Margaret Cranbourne

Food's
awful →

Seafield House
Bishop Petre College

Dear Mum, I've just settled in and i'm the fag to the Head of House, David Fenton-Ryder. He's ever so STRICT but very, fair sometimes. He hit me the other day cause I called Borax 'Borax' and not Mr Baigent. He made me nail all the floorboards down in a VIᵗʰ form study cause he says it's a den of vice. He gave me 3 drills just because I ripped a bit of cloth on the snooker table, and he went beserk when little Robert Huntly broke a window in the dorm with a stool. The stool slipped out of Huntly's hand and Fenton-Ryder says it couldn't fall out of his hand horisontally for 6 metres. Fenton-Ryder said Seafield is the only house worth considering, and if Seefield don't win every cup and prize going he's going to crucify those who don't try. We must win all, even in the Hexads.

There's another boy called Martyn Cranbourne whose got bright ginger hair and greassy spots and he's a real big-head and bullies the first years. He sits in his study and tells the boys along the drive to come to where he's sitting and then he gives them a drill for walking on the grass. Boy was there trouble when Fenton-Ryder saw him doing this. I don't know what happened but Martyn Cranbourne disappeared for nearly 9 week! Someone says they had to operate on him and others say that he hid in the library or sought sanctuary in the chapel. either way, he's no problem now.

The foods awful but Fenton-Ryder says we ought to be grateful for any sustenance.
Fenton-Ryder took three of the fags to the pictures. I quite like him but I wouldn't want to get on the wrong side of him.
Love
Henry.

19 In which Our Hero apprehends a criminal and accidently hospitalises the culprit, and also defends the honour of the school saving his House Tutor from a fate and a shame worse than the most ignoble death.

The first epic is detailed for us by the aid of the local police, who were stunned with the ferocious vigour which Our Hero displayed in his civic duties.

The second great event is outlined by Our Hero himself when he explains to his parents how the highly abusive term 'Ringi' (a nickname given to scholars of Bishop Petre School), caused his blood to stir and his opponents' blood to flow.

POLICE REPORT: SENIOR SGT D. TAYLOR

On your request for information from Police sources
and due to my personal involvement in the incident at
Seafield House last week, I enclose the following exerpts
from the Police reports of the aforesaid incident:

1. Statement from David Fenton-Ryder, pupil

"I was sitting in my study when I heard a loud
crash and shouts. Next moment my friend Herbert bursts
in shouting that he had found some yobbo nicking off
with our tele. I told somebody to ring the Police
while me and Herb chased after the thief. We ran through
the garden and out onto the playing field beyond where we
saw somebody climbing over the road. Then we heard this
crash and when we reached the fence we saw the tele smashed
to pieces on the footpath.
We, me and Herbert were furious. There was no sign
of him, so we started looking down the hedge. Well that
was no good, 'cause we couldn't see anything. So I pinched
this bamboo pole from a garden across the road and poked
it into the hedge. That did the trick. Next moment this
yobbo leaps out of his hiding place and sprints across
the pitch.
I threw the stick but missed. So we chased after
him. Me and Herb must've tackled him at the same time as
he came crashing down and started screaming. Mind you, he
didn't try and run away after that."

2. Initial Report of Findings

On arrival at Seafield House in response to a call, I
was informed that a suspicious person had been chased
towards the vicinity of Rumble Street. I immediately drove
to that vicinity and was hailed from the middle of the
playing fields on the other side of the fence, by two
persons. I left my car and went across to these persons,
who I perceived to be two students standing over a figure
lying on the ground. They told me he was injured and I
realised he needed help, so I called for an ambulance before
questioning the boys. Apparently, in their determination
to catch the suspect, they had tackled him simultaneously
in rugby style, one around the legs, the other around the
waist. In the process, the victim suffered severe injury.

3. Ian Truser, Suspect (aged 19) Unemployed

Admitted to the Central Hospital, 10.30 p.m., June 10,
1983. Duty doctor: Philip Frances.

The patient was complaining of severe pain in his left leg. This was completely understandable since it was fractured just above the knee. However, since he was having problems with all movement I took a closer look. This revealed he had two cracked ribs, also on his left side, and severe bruising to his hips. There was also swelling to his right ankle which I diagnosed as twisted, or maybe torn tissue, it is difficult to be precise at the moment.

The possible explanations for these injuries would be a fall in one direction (probably to his right) and then a forcible push in the opposite direction. This would have to be quite forceful and at the same time as the legs were pinned. The damaged ribs could have been caused by either falling on an object or a blow to the side, but the latter is unlikely since there were no internal injuries.

Conclusion

It seems extraordinary that two boys could cause so much damage to another. I must confess to having been impressed with the prompt and efficient way of dealing with the event. Certainly their helpfulness at all times was a great asset and in no way suggested or hinted at foul play.

Perhaps they might have curbed their enthusiasm and thus prevented a hospital case. But nevertheless it is to their credit that they caught the suspect so efficiently and made our task that much more easy.

I only wish young Fenton-Ryder could spell. He must have used at least a dozen forms before he got it right!

Seafield House

Dear Mother and Father,
                    Thank-you for the long letters they
were very much appreciated. School has been
exciting, despite the fact that my fag can't make
a bed. He's a good lad, although he still has
a lot to learn about the ways of the
school.
        I was involved in a small scandal last
week. The first XV had been playing Boys
High, naturally we won (22-9) and we were
walking back to school. Suddenly we saw a group
of young lads hassling Redmond Pomfritter, we
ran to help him and the yokels had the insolence
to start calling us 'Ringis' and abusing the
name of the school. We made short work
of them and they soon gave up the fight.
        Next morning the police came round inquiring
about why three of the chaps had ended up in
Hospital. When I explained that they had making
a mockery of THE school and Mr. Pommefritter, the
police realised my actions had been justified,
especially as the three wee wanted by the
police anyway.
        Mr. Baigent commended us especially as he
didn't relish the idea of being without a
house tutor.   Yours, love
                           David

20 In which Our Hero, in his final oration to the House, outlines his true philosophy of life, sets the record straight, and in his last line causes his Housemaster some considerable social embarrassment.

The final document is a letter from Our Hero's parents to the Housemaster in which the postscript ruins his holiday, undermines his confidence, and virtually destroys the last remnants of his sanity.

STIRRUP CUP FOR THE LEAVER'S PARENTS

Excerpt from Final Speech

Finally I would like to wish the House all the best for next year.

Seafield's the best House in the School and I'm sure you guys coming back will want to keep it that way. And you will if you all pull together and get on with each other and try hard in everything and do your best; from the first year busting yourselves in a Hexad game; the second year not being sloppy and not whingeing against the officials; the third year getting stuck into sport and work and things; and the senior setting a good example all the time and being loyal.

We're lucky with our Housemaster. Mr Baigent is always interested in all of us and is always fair. I know all the leavers join me in thanking Mr and Mrs Baigent for all they have done for us during our time in Seafield.

Now I ask the leavers to rise and drink the health of the returners: To the Housemaster and his Mistress and all those returning next year.

GLENDALE STATION

GORDONSDOWN

New Zealand

December 12th

Dear Tony,

Bryan and I did so enjoy staying with you and Peggie for the end of year break-up. What a super idea to ask the Head of House's parents to stay in Seafield for the occasion. We were so proud of David at the House Supper and were absolutely amazed that he could speak so fluently.

Your drinks party after the Prize Giving was tremendous fun. Did feel so sorry for Peggie with her headache having to stand for that interminable time listening to Margo Cranbourne screeching at the top of her voice about what she thought was wrong with the school. That woman wasn't even blessed with tact as compensation for her absence of brainpower.

Bryan and I would again like to express our sincere appreciation for all you have done for David in the past five years. We feel he goes out into the world a young man any parent would be proud of.

Our fond good wishes to you and Peggie for Xmas and the New Year.

Affectionately,
Cynthia.

P.S. Really looking forward to our second-born, Richard, starting at Seafield next year. Bryan & I feel it only fair to warn you that Ricky is not the easy cooperative child that David was at the same age.

C.

Borax: Post Postscript!!

GLOSSARY

(Notes by Fenton-Ryder.)

Bach	Holiday home — *heaven*
Big School	Main teaching area & Assembly Hall. — *Hell*
Blueshirt	Senior Prefect. — *Servants of Hell*
Bursary	Senior Public Examination — *ugh*
Common Room	Staff area — *Hades*
D of E	Duke of Edinburgh's Award Scheme. *and punishment*
Dorm	Dormitory. *riot house*
Fag	Junior boy to assist Senior. — *Slavery*
Grace	Period of time for new boys to make mistakes without being punished. — *to be made the most of*
Gated	Not allowed out of School. — *often!*
Hexads	Minor sports (soft ball etc) — *Communist plot*
House Tutor	Master assisting House Master. — *you get all sorts!*
Initiation Ceremonies	As it stands. — *No comment*
The Lodge	School outdoors building.
Matron	*Grand*Motherly-type lady resident in House.
Prep	Homework. *damn nuisance*
Pink Slip	Weekly report slip for naughty boys. — *I hold the record*
Porro Pueri Caligis Ipsis	School motto . . . "In Boys Boots and all."
Repeats	Redoing Prep. — *especially damn nuisance*
UE	University Entrance Examination. *??*
7D	Form for those clever enough to miss their 6th Form. *CREEPS*
Studies	Individual rooms for senior boys. *smoking lounges*
School Cert	5th year public examination. — *easy*
Tardy	Punishment for being late. (e.g. reporting to HM's house at 6.30 am) — *yet another personal best*
Ticket	Punishment for being untidy *ditto*
Turd	1st year *Peasants, untouchables, weeds, Maggots*
Weta	Nasty large New Zealand Insect. *Beautiful !!!*